MAKING PAPER COSTUMES

MAKING PAPER COSTUMES

Janet Boyes

Publishers **Plays Inc.** *Boston*

Copyright © Janet Boyes 1974

First American edition published by Plays, Inc 1974

Reprinted 1980

**Library of Congress Cataloging
in Publication Data**

Boyes, Janet.
Making paper costumes.

Summary: Instructions for making, decorating, and
fireproofing paper costumes for both younger and
older children.

1 Costume – Juvenile literature. 2 Paper work –
Juvenile literature. [1 Costume. 2 Paper work]
I. Title.

TT633.B69 1973   646.4′7   73–5841
ISBN 0–8238–0147–0

Printed in the United States of America

CONTENTS

Introduction   7
Safety   11

Experimental projects   12
For younger children   12
For older children   15
Experiments with the quality
of the materials   20

Linking paper units   21

**Studying movement
of the body**   35
Paper costumes allowing for movement   36

**Inspiration from
historical costume**   37
Sculpture inspired
by an Elizabethan costume   41

Costume construction   43

Bodice details   72

Head coverings   76

Hand coverings   80
Decoration   84
Points to remember   84

Costumes in PVC   85
Suppliers   88

ACKNOWLEDGMENT

I would like to thank the following for their valuable and willing help in the preparation of this book: the recent students from the Foundation Studies Course at West Sussex College of Design, Worthing; the boys and girls of St Mary's Roman Catholic School, St Andrew's High School for Boys, and the Davison High School for Girls, Worthing.

I am indebted to Derek Barcock, Eric Cleavely and Fred Hampton for their excellent photography which has greatly enhanced the book; and to my friend Margaret Bibby for the photographs of her freestanding sculpture.

My special thanks to Barry Purchese for all his help in compiling the text, and for his constant encouragement and advice.

INTRODUCTION

Paper is a familiar substance in everyday use. We use it to write on, for printing, painting and drawing. It is plasticized, surface textured, coated and metallicized. It is also used for interior decoration in the home and is usually wrapped around our everyday shopping.

Perhaps the display packaging industry has come nearest to understanding the full potential of the various weights, surface textures and coatings of cards and papers, many of which can be obtained in shops which stock artists' materials. Large department stores, particularly at Christmas and Easter, use a wide variety of ingenious cardboard and paper structures, both for the decoration of the store and for their packaging displays.

Until recently, the plastics industry has dealt almost exclusively with products such as lightweight, interlocking, fold-away furniture for children. The last few years, however, have seen the emergence of paper and cardboard castles, houses and robots which can be constructed and dismantled without specialist knowledge, or fear of injury, and which are sufficiently robust to ensure a reasonable life span for the financial outlay involved.

Until now, the dress industry has only used paper material in the cut and style which lends itself to traditional methods of manufacture. The majority of paper dresses produced have imitated the cheap cotton, easily laundered dress, but lacked a sufficiently competitive price to make it the more favoured of the two. Low-priced garments are only a commercial proposition when they can be produced in very large quantities, in a simple and easily assembled style. Thus, we saw an exciting new material discarded after one season on the market because its properties, potential and acceptability has not been fully realised and tested. We saw an over publicised, under-developed product, in this case the paper dress, prove a commercial flop and disappear.

However, disposable paper utility garments such as surgical masks and helmets, underwear, bibs and aprons have fully exploited the characteristic short life of the material and have enjoyed a certain amount of success.

Although we have seen the items described, if not in direct use, then through the various advertising media, we have not yet seen paper being used as an exploratory clothing medium, which breaks away from the traditional concepts of covering the human body and provides both educational stimuli and great enjoyment for people of all ages and abilities, by offering different ways of manipulating the material and assembling the final costume.

The mental attitude of each person undertaking the task of creating a paper packaging in the form of costume is essentially important. Is efficiency the key word in the operation, or warmth; is it flexibility, or dynamic impact?

By doubting pre-conceived ideas about clothing, one can begin to construct a body covering which forms its own structural aesthetics, through the ingenuity in manipulating the many different types of paper and card.

This book describes how groups of young people were encouraged to explore the qualities of such materials, to examine the problems relating to making paper costumes, and to develop their own creative solutions. Although these experiments were carried out as team efforts and in restricted periods of time, anyone working alone and at their own pace will be equally benefitted by the exercises which the students conducted and the lessons which they learned. It is hoped that many readers will want to practise these ideas not only for educational purposes, or for dramatic use, but for their own pleasure.

Certain clarifications should be made before attempting to construct any complex paper covering.

1   It is important to determine the purpose for which the garments are being made.

Are the garments to be produced as part of creative play, or an educational programme for people of any age and ability?

Are the coverings being produced for a specific theatrical production, or are they being produced to show variation of technique in the handling and assembling of many different types of paper?

2   Determine what materials are available and in what quantities. These can be sub-divided into materials which would have to be purchased and material which could be found.

In the list of materials below, it is by no means necessary to purchase the expensive items in quantity. It is the *variety* of materials that is most important, as opposed to their cost, quality or quantity.

Materials to purchase
Cartridge papers of mixed colours
Sugar papers of mixed colours
Card in various weights and colours
Wallpapers of any type or colour
Vinyl-backed papers
Flocked wallpapers
Kitchen foil, paper cups, doilies, etc.
Metallized card
Acetate
Cellophane
Mellinex
Vilene

Materials to find
General purpose wrapping paper
Paper bags of various sizes and thicknesses
Tissue paper fruit wrappings
Paper and vinyl egg boxes
Corrugated card
Newspapers
Cardboard boxes
String

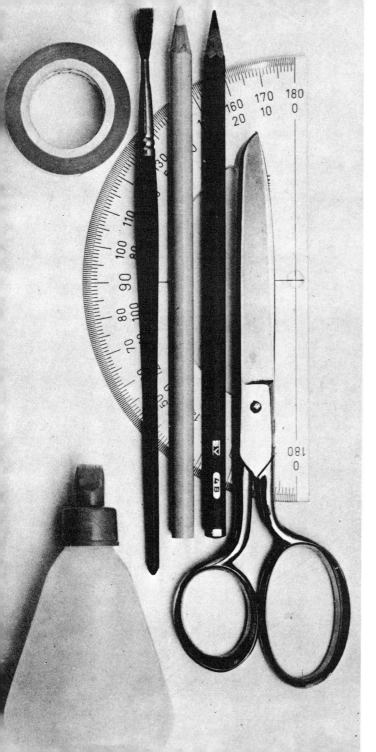

3 Sort out the equipment available for use. Again a variety of items is far more important than quality or quantity. The most essential items are those which are italicized.

Scissors
Cutting blade
Stapler with staples
Straight pins and safety pins
Paper adhesive
Paints
Brushes
Crayons
Household aerosol paints

Hole punch
String, of different strengths
Transparent adhesive tape
  (*Sellotape, Scotch Tape*)
Pinking shears
Pencils
Ruler
Protractor
Pair of compasses

4 Decide whether it is to be a group project, or an individual effort.

In a teaching situation, the teacher will have to ascertain age, capabilities and time allocation. These will have a direct bearing on the type and amount of work that can be tackled.

5 Before making the costume, experiment with the papers, cards and tools which have been gathered together. This enables each person to experience the nature of each type of card and paper and how they can best be manipulated.

Questions concerning the strain that each sort of paper can withstand, or the most successful ways of joining together different types, shapes

d weights of paper are best answered before
e garment is begun.

Examine, measure and draw the body which
going to be covered, or indeed any human
gure, in order to grasp the complexities of how
e body structure alters during movement. If
e garment is to be worn for a dramatic
roduction, certain parts of the body may be
mphasised and other parts played down if
esired.

In order to reconstruct a period costume in
aper, a full working knowledge of the body
ovement is essential, in order that an accurate,
mplified translation from the original can be
onstructed, which would accurately reflect the
ood and line of the particular period chosen.

afety

ertain points relating to safety should be
bserved at all times. With young children in
articular, the use and storage of cutting blades
d sharp-ended scissors should be approached
ith caution. Care should be taken if facial
overings or masks are to be made to avoid
uffocation of the model. There is always a small
re risk, and perhaps this is at its greatest when
aper costumes are being used in a dramatic
roduction, and people around the actors may be
mpted to smoke. A certain amount of fire
esistance can be achieved by dipping or spraying
e flat sheets of paper on both sides with a flame
roofing solution, before the sheets are cut into
eir various shapes. Flame proofing crystals can
e purchased at a dispensing chemist's and should
e made up into a strong solution of 1 part
rystals to four parts tepid water. When the

crystals are dissolved the solution can then be
applied to the paper by a hand squeeze spray or a
hand pressurised spray. The paper should be
allowed to dry thoroughly before using. A damp
sheet of cartridge paper which has curled after
spraying can be successfully ironed flat with a
warm iron.

Fireproof paints can be purchased at most
large paint stockists and are available in a wide
range of colours.

Cardboard should be sprayed on both sides as
opposed to dipping and all surfaces of both card
and paper should be tested with the solution
before the spraying of any large area takes place.

Mellinex and *vilene* have a flame resistant
surface and these two fabrics together with pvc
and acetate should not be sprayed before using.

The creators of the costumes should bear in
mind that cardboard and paper have sharp edges,
and care should be taken to avoid cutting either
the maker or the wearer.

EXPERIMENTAL PROJECTS

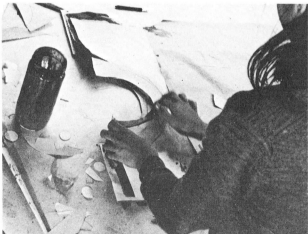

1, 2

1–6   Making costumes using disposable paper sacks

For younger children

The following photographs show the results of a day-long project involving boys and girls whose ages ranged between seven and nine years. The materials and equipment used were based on a selected variety from the lists given in the previous section, with the addition of adhesive shapes and disposable paper sacks, which measured approximately 1 m × 40 cm (3 ft × 1 ft 4 in.).

Following a fairly brief description of the different materials and equipment which could be used, newsprint, adhesive shapes and cartridge paper were chosen with which to construct the first garment. Then, after a short demonstration of sticking, stapling and paint spraying, the children were asked to produce one completed paper garment.

The children worked in pairs to construct a garment which would fit one of them and in this way they came to grips with the problems of measurement, of getting garments on and off without tearing and of placing the armholes in the correct position in order for the arms to slot through.

The results and frustrated cries of this particular work period appeared to prove that the three-quarters of an hour spent on a preliminary session was far more effective than a detailed description of the problems which could arise, issued by the teacher.

3

For the second project, disposable paper sacks were used for the main shape and each child was asked to produce one garment, covering or tunic, to fit himself or herself.

A great deal of enthusiasm, excitement and energy was exerted during the working time.

Manipulation of the equipment and materials appeared to present little or no difficulty. There was obvious enjoyment expressed in each child being able to wear his or her own paintings and shapes as an almost instant and personal form of clothing.

The afternoon session proved to be even more enjoyable, when each boy and girl was asked to turn themselves into an imaginary animal or bird, by using the paper sacks as the main covering material. The garments were completed within one and a half hours.

4, 5

6

For older children

Older children tackled the problems of making paper costumes in an entirely different way.

The materials and equipment used are listed below

Materials

Card
Cartridge paper (different colours)
Sugar paper (mixed colours)
Kitchen foil
Adhesive metallic papers
Strips of PVC (textured and plain)

Equipment

Stapler and staples
Scissors
Cutting blades
Hole punch
String

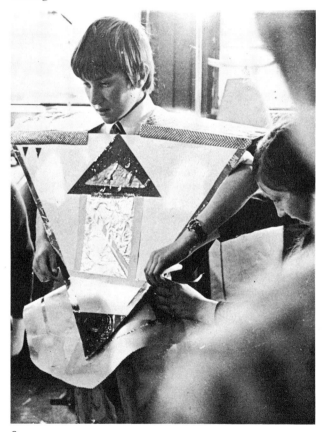

–14   Making costumes based on the circle, square and triangle

8

Sellotape and adhesive
Aerosol household paints
Pencils
Compass and rulers

Five boys and five girls aged between twelve and fourteen were split up into groups and one covering was to be produced from each group and worn by one of its members. The children were asked to base the entire body covering and applied decoration on either the square, triangle or circle shape.

After talking about the materials and equipment which could be used, each group attempted to resolve their combined ideas by discussing and drawing out their solutions to the problem. They soon found it necessary to simplify some of the more complex shapes which

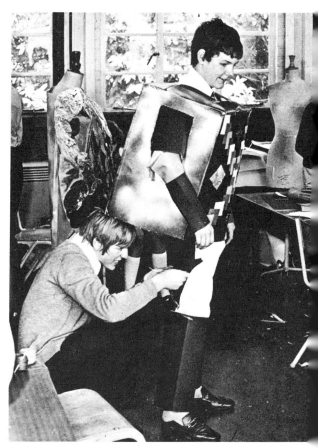

9

10

sprang from the adventurous but impractical ideas of one or two of the members.

It was interesting to hear, not only the co-operation between members of each group but also the criticism voiced on the craftmanship, colour choice and speed of manufacture from one group member to another.

A great deal of excitement was generated towards the end of the session when the finishing touches were being applied to the various sections of the costumes.

The results of both the school projects demonstrated that the wearing of the final costume proved every bit as important to the children as the basic conception, construction and decoration involved in creating each outfit.

The very familiar shapes used, such as the circle, square and triangle, together with their

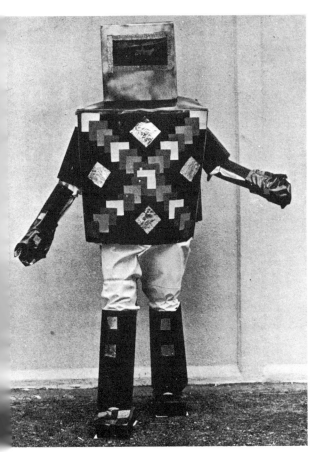

12

13

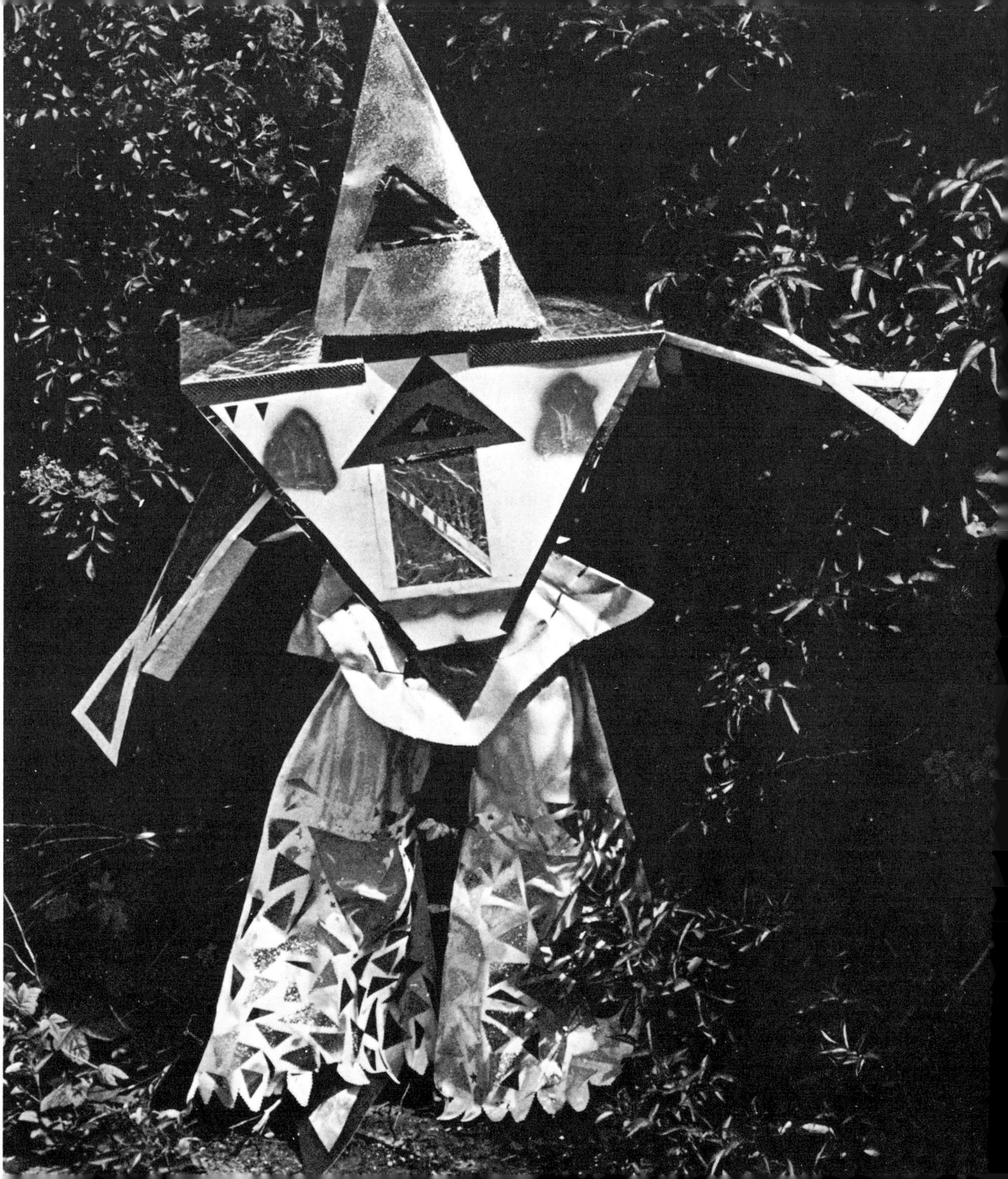

resulting costumes, indicated that many other geometric shapes which could have been chosen such as the rectangle, rhombus or elipse, etc, would probably have led to equally adventurous results.

In the first project the product was a fantasy animal; it might equally well have been an insect, bird or human character. The costume might have been made to express a mood such as anger or greed; or there might have been a stylistic theme such as the use of fringes. There are many permutations from which to choose. At all times the student must work out his or her own individual solution to the problem.

The solutions to building and fitting the costume structure should be as flexible as possible in order to allow the children to realise fully the problems which will constantly arise.

Experiments with the quality of the materials

The importance of experimenting with the many different varieties of paper and card, before beginning the full construction of a costume, cannot be over-emphasised. The purpose of this is to find out as much as possible about the materials at hand, in the hope of preventing a disaster at a later stage in the development of the costume. It also serves to give each person involved in this type of activity a greater awareness of the many possibilities open to their individual exploitation.

The following brief was given to students of seventeen to eighteen years at the beginning of an experimental session:

> Familiarise yourselves with every possible type of paper-based material you can find. The paper need not be bought and in a flat sheet but sought for around the community wherever packaging is disposed of. Find as many types of paper and card as possible and then try to tear it, screw it up, wet it and stretch it, mould it, lacerate it and fray it. You could weave it and fold it, compare each different type for its tensile strength and comparative weight. Try simple folding and intersectioning, and at no time rely upon staples or adhesives. In short, experiment fully and find out all you can.

The students were reminded that the shape, size, and strength of the object produced should echo the quality of the paper or card from which it has been constructed. It was also suggested that after using adhesives in the initial stages, as the creative process became more involved and each student more familiar with the materials, adhesives should be discarded in favour of structural bending and folding. By doing this it was hoped that a greater understanding of the complexities and the capabilities of the medium could be achieved.

This period of activity proved to be exciting, enjoyable and of great value, as the shapes that were finally arrived at began to show how strong or how weak one particular type of card could be under different conditions.

All the objects that had been produced, whether successes or failures, were presented for an open discussion at the end of the experimental period.

'It is incredible to discover that a strip of flimsy paper could be folded in such a way as to give it the strength to withstand two people pulling on either end of it.'

'I would never have believed that sugar paper was made in so many layers.'

'My hands are blistered from cutting corrugated card.'

'Tissue paper knits very well.'

'I didn't realise that wet tracing paper was so easy to mould over a textured surface.'

'I'm covered in the dye colour which ran out of the wet tissue paper!'

LINKING PAPER UNITS

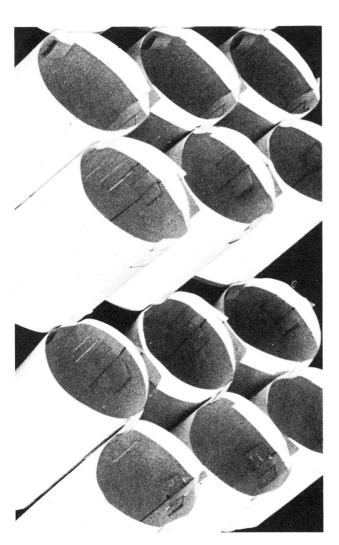

Once aware of the many qualities of the different materials, it is possible to tackle more specific problems. This time the same group of students were to use their ingenuity in applying this newly-acquired experience to achieve a pre-determined end product. Their assignment was:

Devise and construct, through bending piercing and interlocking, without the use of staples or any adhesives, a unit in paper. This unit must be capable of joining with another identical unit in any direction, again without adhesives. Thus, a string of units can be joined in blanket form. This paper blanket has to be capable of covering a part of the body which is subjected to continual movement and has to allow a maximum of flexibility at all times.

It was necessary at the beginning of this work period to clarify the many different ways of linking different pieces of paper and card together, in order to give a stable and satisfactory fastening, before the actual unit could be constructed.

There are many ways of linking different shapes and types of paper. The easiest and most successful are the tab and slot devices which are illustrated.

Many sophisticated units and methods of linking them together were devised, and although more than sixty students attempted this particular problem, each produced a different result.

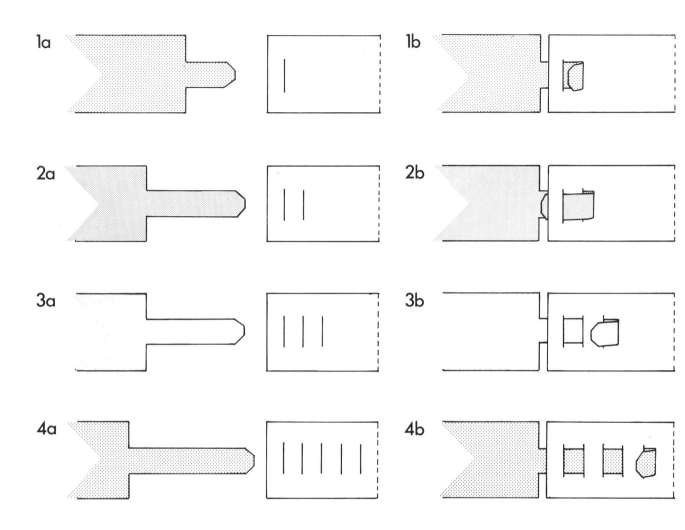

Diagrams 1 to 4   Examples of single to five slot methods of linking which can be used to join two different pieces of paper together

Diagrams 5 to 8   Variations of simple tabs and slot linking with diagrams 6 to 8 giving a more flexible joint than diagram 5

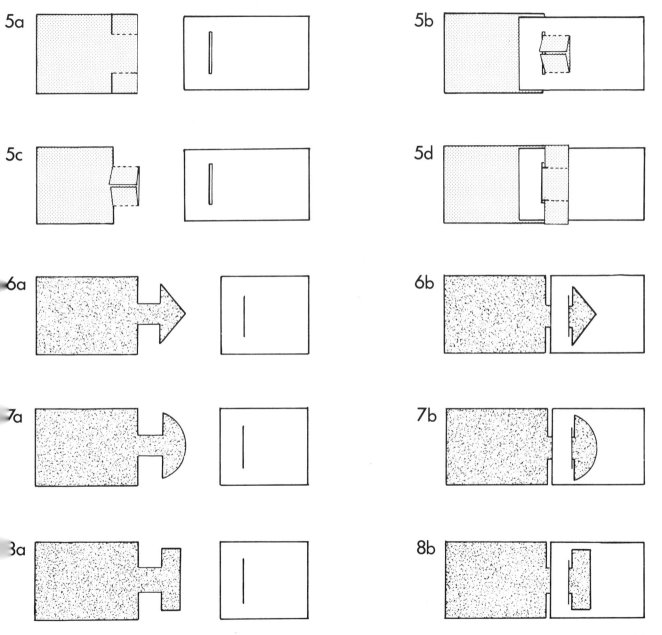

5a

5b

5c

5d

6a

6b

7a

7b

8a

8b

23

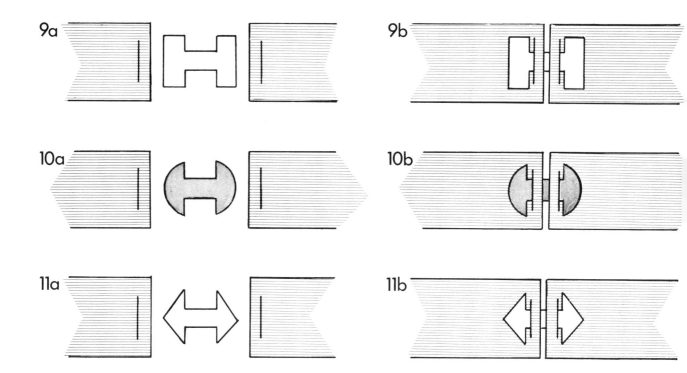

Diagrams 9 to 11   A method of linking paper or
card by introducing a separate linking unit

24

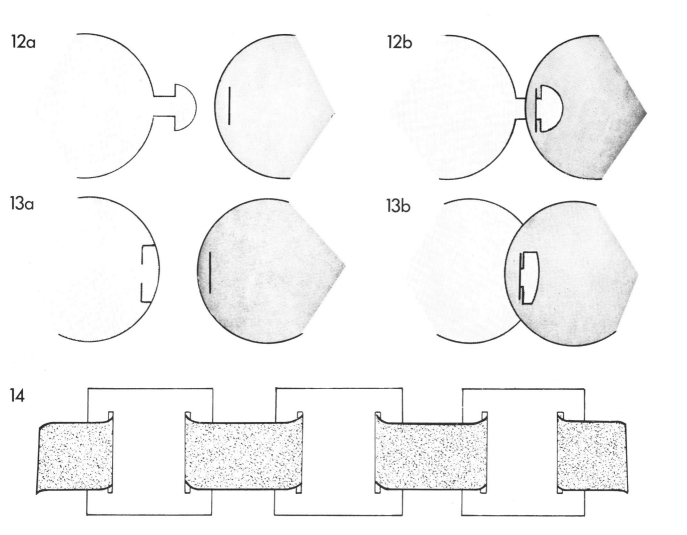

12a

12b

13a

13b

14

Diagrams 12 and 13   Different methods of joining
circular or curved shapes
Diagram 12 keeps the full shape intact and 13
creates an overlapping structure

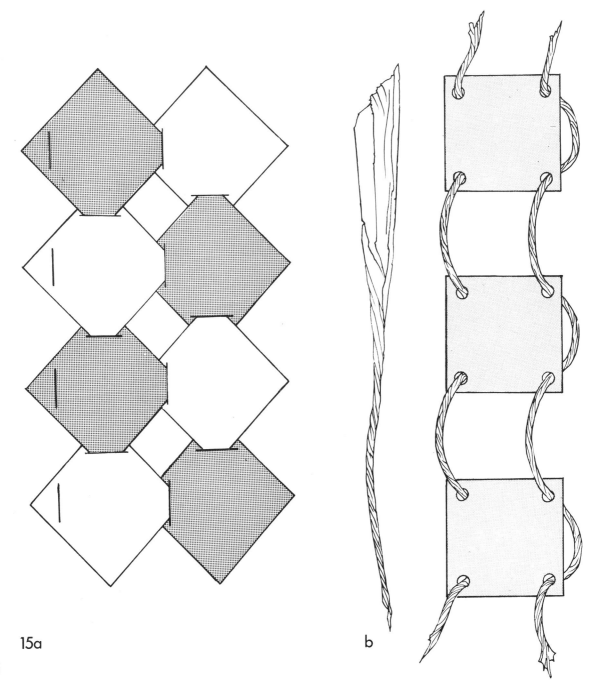

15a

b

Diagram 15   Simple methods of linking square paper units together. In (a) by inserting the corner of the square into the corresponding slot and in (b) by twisting a strip of fine weight paper to form a length of paper 'string' which can then be used to lace the squares of paper or card together

Diagram 16   Construction of a unit formed by intersecting circles. The notches are then marked and cut as indicated on the diagram. By making a cardboard template of the original unit, many more units can be reproduced quickly and then linked together in a long chain

16

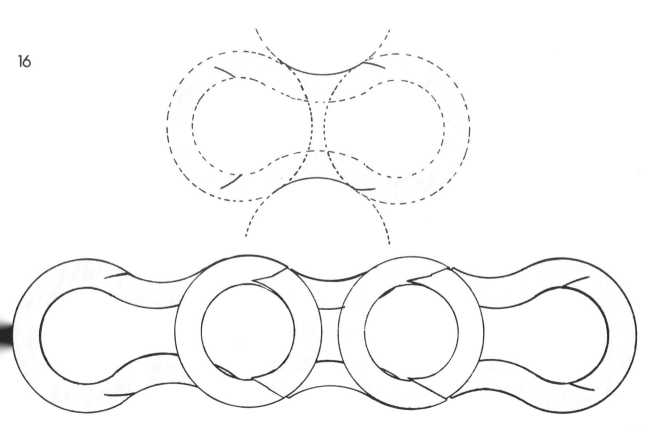

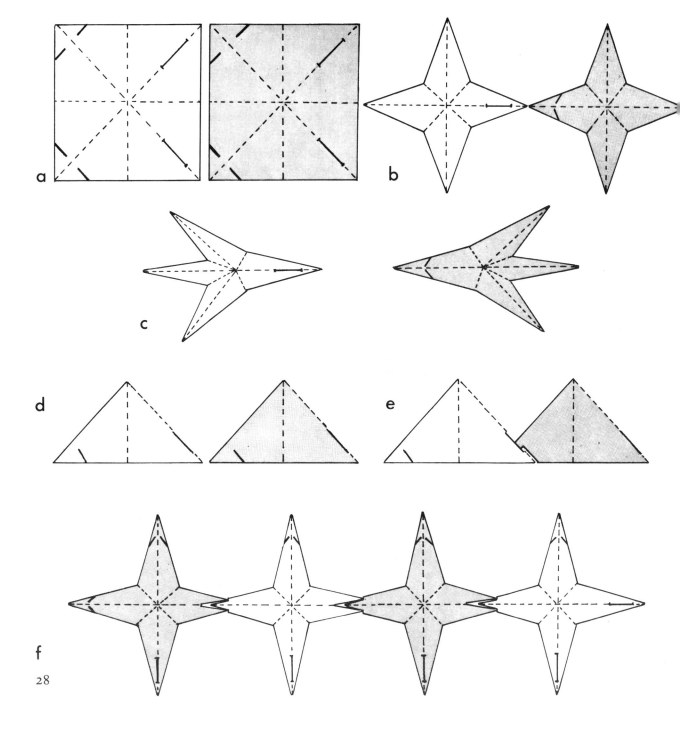

agram 17   A step by step construction of a star
aped flexible cartridge paper blanket. A very
nple slot linking device has been successfully
ployed here. Figure 15 illustrates a three
nensional construction of the unit

a

b

c

30

d

a

60°

60°

b

c

f

diagrams 18 and 19   Units which can be constructed
out of cartridge paper of any colour or quality. The
drawing is to half scale. The first unit should be
constructed in card and cut out very carefully with a
sharp blade or scissors. This will then act as a
template for drawing round and thereby, the means
for quick construction of other identical units

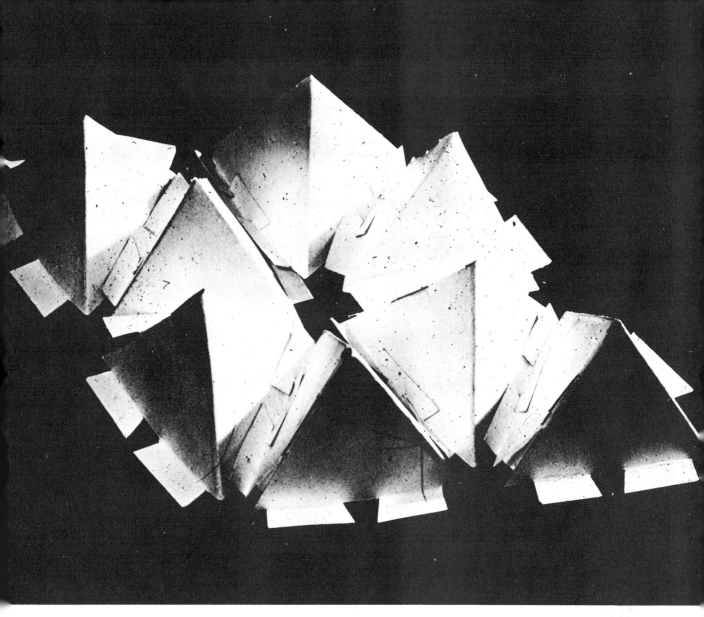

5 An interesting solution to the 'linking paper
nits' problem. This unit can be linked horizontally
r vertically and is constructed in cartridge paper

above

17 A pyramid like unit constructed in fine card

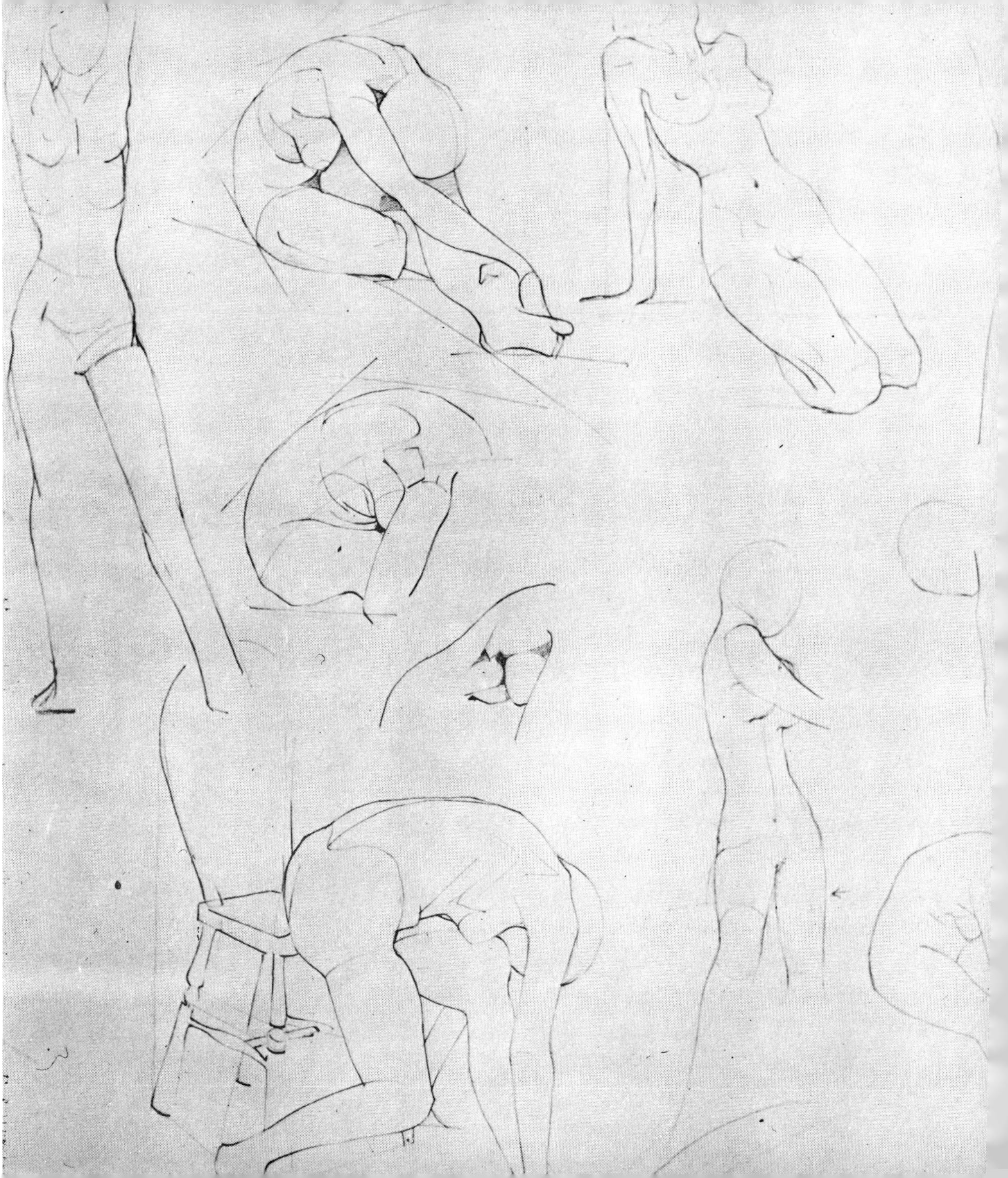

STUDYING MOVEMENT OF THE BODY

When attempting to create a covering for the body, which when moving is a highly complex mechanical object, it is essential that one has an understanding of the body's flexibility. Great emphasis should be placed on constant drawing practice, in order that acute observation of a body undergoing movement and stress can be fully observed and critically and objectively documented by a series of marks. These marks should show the distribution of weight or the tension in a body which has been 'frozen' in a particular pose, or is moving very slowly.

It is extremely beneficial to get a life model to hold poses for thirty seconds, under tension, and then move slowly around the room, twisting and bending but 'freezing' the action at various stages.

Students should move around the model discussing the stress points of the muscles and joints and then, very simply, with a limited number of pencil marks, to avoid the confusion of lines, try to capture the essence of the pose and the force of the tension.

Often it is helpful for the students themselves to experience the feelings of a pose under tension, and then to try and relate their feelings of stress in visual terms, again with a minimum of lines or marks. These self-inflicted poses help the student to come to grips with the problems of movement at first hand, rather than dealing with what appears to be happening in front of them.

Each student can then begin to relate the sight with the feeling.

Models are not always easily available so students could take turns in modelling for short sessions. With a clothed model and a similar series of poses, the visual results are just as convincing as those achieved when a nude model is used.

This type of study is essential for a person who eventually has to successfully resolve covering the human body with any type of material, because allowances have to be made to permit adequate movement to take place. Even if the drawing periods with the model are short, or conducted at spasmodic intervals, it will still be seen that those who have pursued this activity are at a far greater advantage when it comes to embarking upon the final construction of the body covering, than those who have not.

The illustrations show working drawings from this analytical movement study and it is obvious that an understanding of the flexibility of the human form has been achieved.

opposite
18 Examples of working drawings from an analytical movement study

35

Paper costumes allowing for movement

Once the problem of making linked paper units has been solved, and the preliminary study of body movement has been made, it is possible to start constructing a costume for someone who will be moving about whilst wearing it. This was tackled by a group of seventeen and eighteen year olds who started with the following brief:

> Working as a team of two or three people, *forget* about all pre-conceived ideas of clothing and flexibility and, using the knowledge you have gained about the movement of the body, cover the entire body in paper or card, allowing maximum movement. This operation has to be carried out without the use of staples or or adhesives.

How does one set about fully covering the body using paper or card? If working in a group or team, it is best for each member to establish his or her own ideas and then throw them open to the group for acceptance or, possibly, rejection.

After each team has chosen one member to model the costume, the initial task should concern the measuring of the body area which has to be covered. The first set of measurements should be taken while the model stands in a relaxed position and then the relevant sections of the body should be measured whilst the model is bending or stretching.

The garment or covering could be an amalgamation of ideas from independent group members, brought together by linking one person's section to the next. In this way an entire covering could be unified by colour or by adopting the interlocking unit method which has been described earlier. The group may agree upon a common unit which would be capable of being reproduced in varying scales, depending upon the measurements structure and movements of those parts of the body which it was intended to cover.

An eight-hour working period offers the chance to explore the use of different coloured cards and papers and the transparency of different types of tissue and tracing papers.

By using different lighting situations in conjunction with fluorescent colours and foil-backed cards, some extremely interesting shapes could be formed by the light and shadows. Imagine the impact of seeing the 'models' moving under a strong white light or under ultra-violet lighting, or camouflaged by colour projection.

It is possible to combine flat sheets of household PVC kitchen foil and metallic coated papers and vinyls with ordinary paper and card. By manipulating these materials in exactly the same way as paper, that is, without the use of stapling or adhesives, but by folding, intersecting, and linking it together, the added effect of reflection can be achieved, on part or the whole covering for the body.

It is the planning and the discussion stage that is most important when using these additional materials, as each structure and different reflective surface must create a total image when all are gathered together on the final costume.

INSPIRATION FROM HISTORICAL COSTUME

The Elizabethan court dress is based on a detail of a sixteenth century painting showing the Coronation procession of Queen Elizabeth I.

The front bodice is constructed of medium weight card which takes the weight of the pleated cartridge ruff. This is attached to the bodice by staples at the front, top right and top left of the bodice section.

9, 20   Basic construction

The bodice straps, which are fastened at the centre back, are also attached by staples to the front bodice, below and behind where the pleated ruff has been joined. Holes are punched in the ends of these straps and threaded with string which is tied in bow fastenings.

The back bodice is an independent section. Its height is determined by the height of the ruff as its purpose is to prevent the ruff from falling backwards. The shoulder width is designed to create the classical wide shoulder line of the Elizabethan period.

The sleeves of cartridge paper are held together across the shoulders by a rectangular strip of folded paper which is stapled to the top of each sleeve section. The sleeves are based on the paper Chinese lantern principle.

The front and back of the skirts are identical.

The top skirt section is made up of two almost semi-circular pieces of medium-weight card, covered in cartridge paper, with an attached waist band. Both sections are punched with holes and joined together by string which is tied with bows.

The bottom skirt section is made of folded sections of cartridge paper, slotted together around the top of the fold and held by a spot of adhesive at the bottom of the skirt. Holes have been punched in between each fold which correspond to the holes in the almost circular sections of the top skirt. The bottom skirt has been looped to the top skirt section by string which is again tied into bows.

The shaped coronet is made of medium-weight card and is joined by adhesive to a card headband. It is fastened at the back of the head by string.

For the decoration aerosol household paints have been sprayed through paper doilies, on the main bodice, skirt and top sleeve sections. Cut-out doily shapes, both sprayed and plain, have been applied with adhesive to the coronet, ruff, bodice, skirt and sleeve sections. Crushed tissue paper has been pushed into the spacious sections of the sleeves and pulled through the slits, in order to achieve the effect of 'slashing' which is a typical sixteenth century tailoring technique. The circular motif was chosen for its Elizabethan characteristic, the painted, lace-like edging for its fineness, and rolled silver foil applied to the coronet with adhesive, to give the effect of pearls.

The colours used on the costume were metallic silver and metallic copper.

Before embarking upon the reconstruction of any period costume it is advisable to make a simplified drawing from the reference material, and to turn back frequently to the drawing and the original, if possible, throughout the process of the construction.

opposite and overleaf
21, 22 The costume after the decoration has been applied

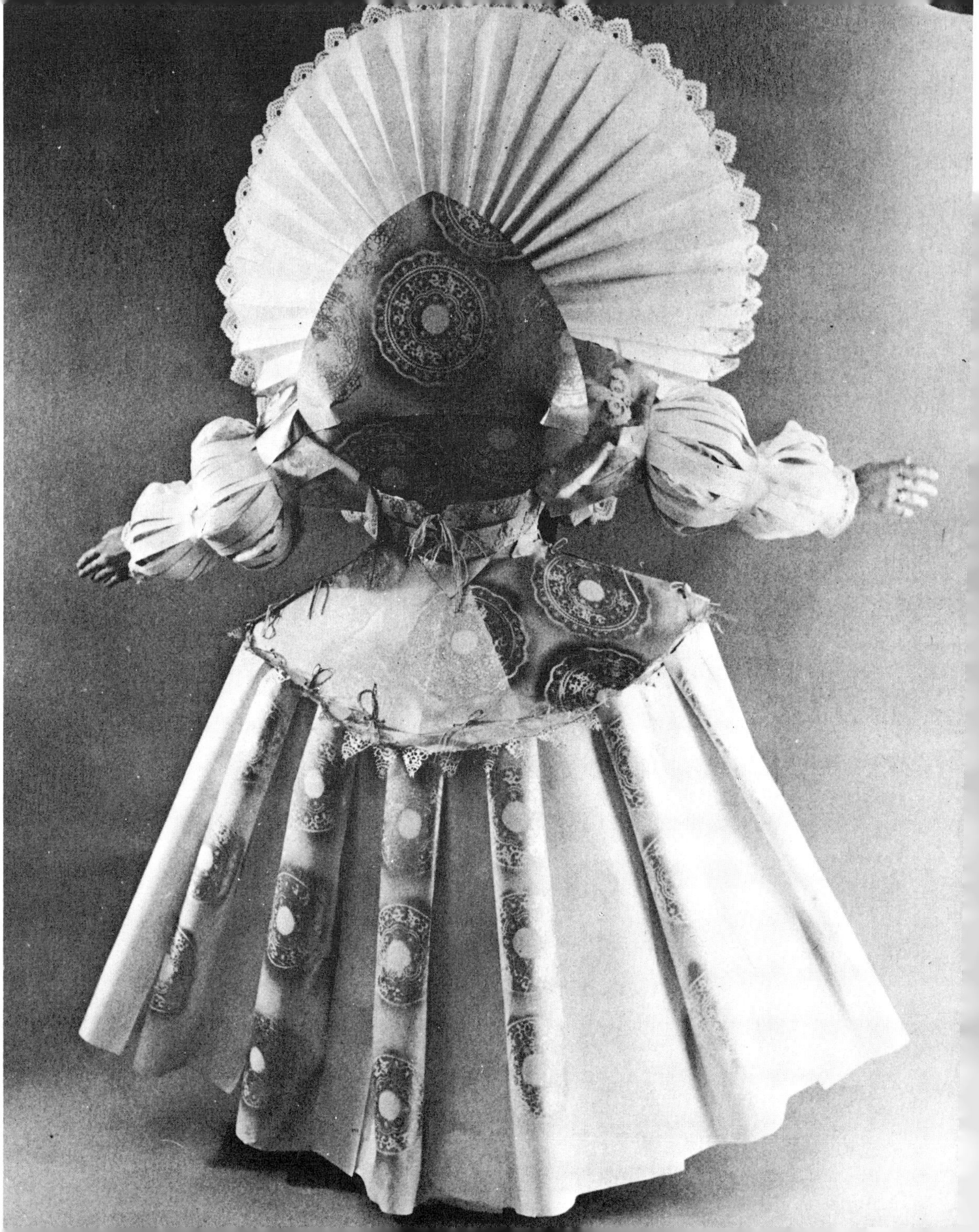

bove and overleaf
3, 24   The construction is on full sized human
cale

Sculpture inspired by an Elizabethan costume

The following illustrations show an experiment by a student of sculpture. This involved using fine card and padded material to achieve a stylised static object, which has the look of a period costume but is unable to be worn.

An old theatrical costume provided both the inspiration and the fabrics for the making of the object. The style has been simplified, but although the fabric has been re-constituted and padded, it has nevertheless been used in the same relationship and quantities as on the original garment.

The loose pleating of the original skirt has been regulated into symmetrical cardboard pleating, which gives the object balance and at the same time retains an early sixteenth century formality about it.

Capturing the feeling of a particular period and translating the line of that period with a certain degree of accuracy into a paper costume, can create certain problems. However, by experimenting with different types of papers and card before embarking on the final work, those materials that will carry the folds, translate flimsiness, or give a controlled line, will soon become apparent.

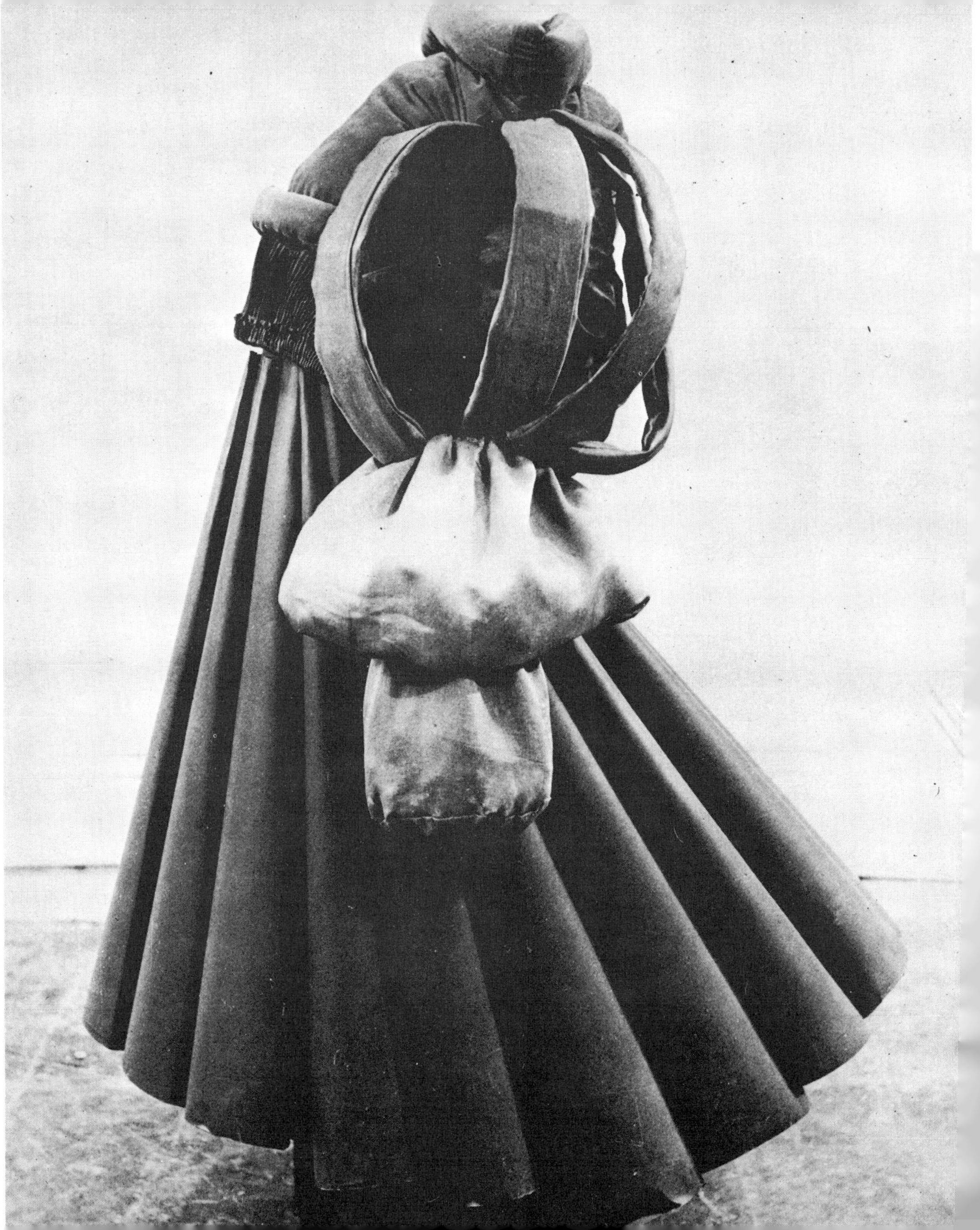

COSTUME CONSTRUCTION

a

b

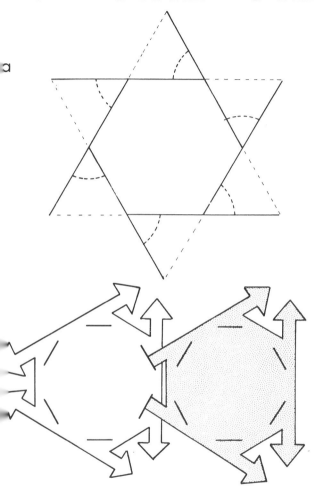

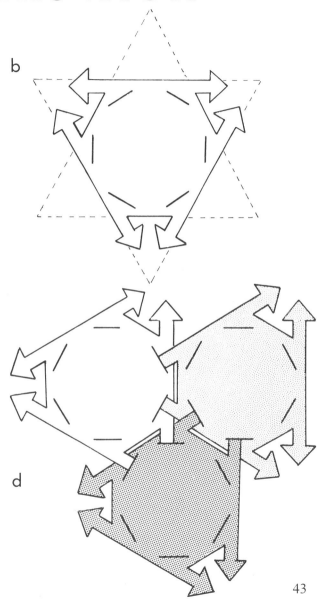

d

Diagram 20 Step by step construction of a unit in
paper which has been used as the 'fabric' for the
sleeves in a garment constructed from two types of
'linking paper units'

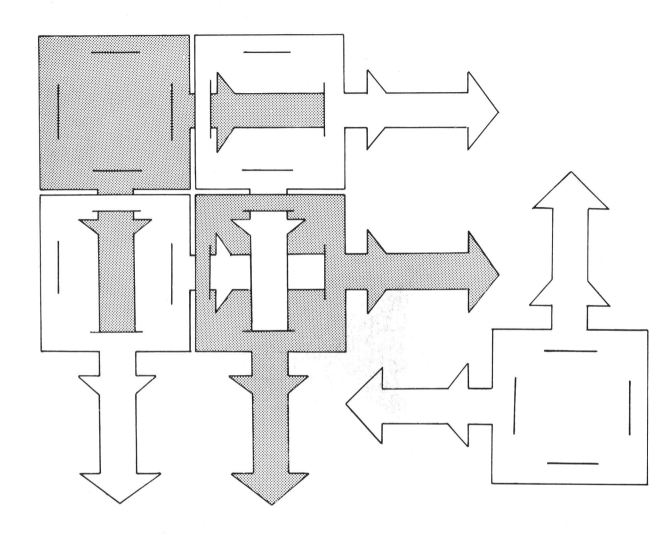

opposite
Plate 1   An experiment in using fluorescent papers to form a multi-coloured tabard and helmet, to be word specifically under ultra-violet lighting. See page 68

Diagram 21   The unit and its method of linking, which has been used for the rest of the garment

overleaf
25   The full scale construction

25

45

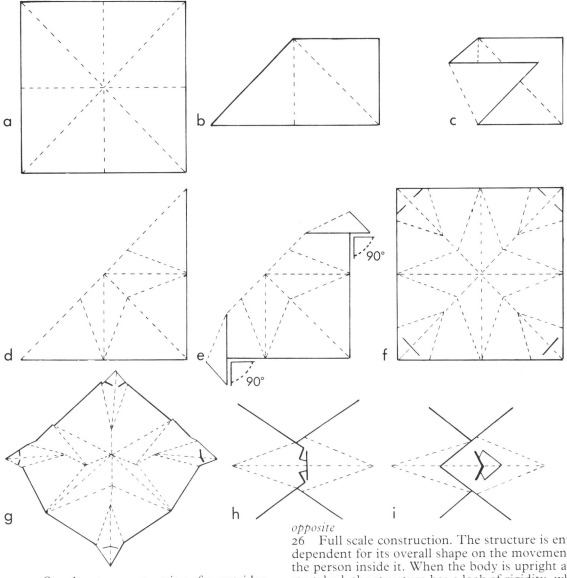

Diagram 22   Step by step construction of a cartridge paper unit, which has been used to make a complete body covering

opposite
26   Full scale construction. The structure is entire dependent for its overall shape on the movement of the person inside it. When the body is upright and stretched, the structure has a look of rigidity, when the body is relaxed, or bending, the structure folds and drapes like a very full cloak

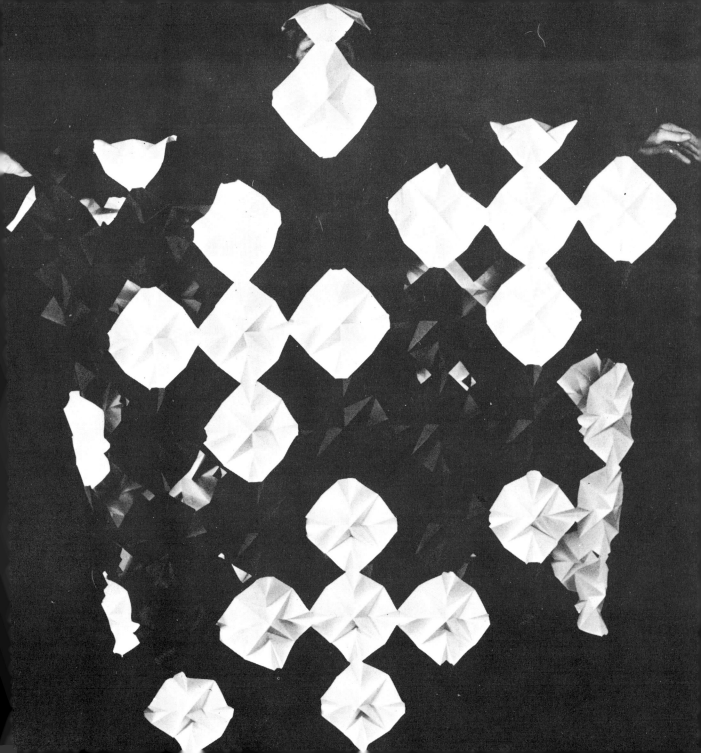

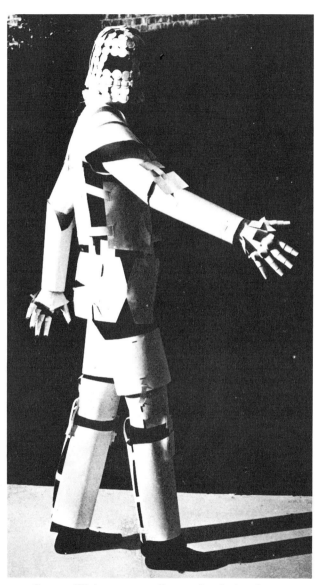
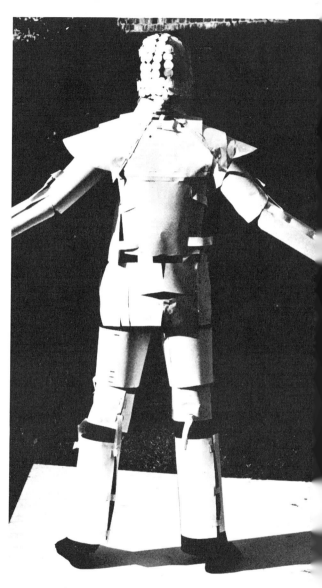

27, 28, 29 This garment shows clearly by the variety of shapes, that different people have tackled different sections of the body and united the structure by each using identical material, which in this case is cartridge paper, and one overall colour

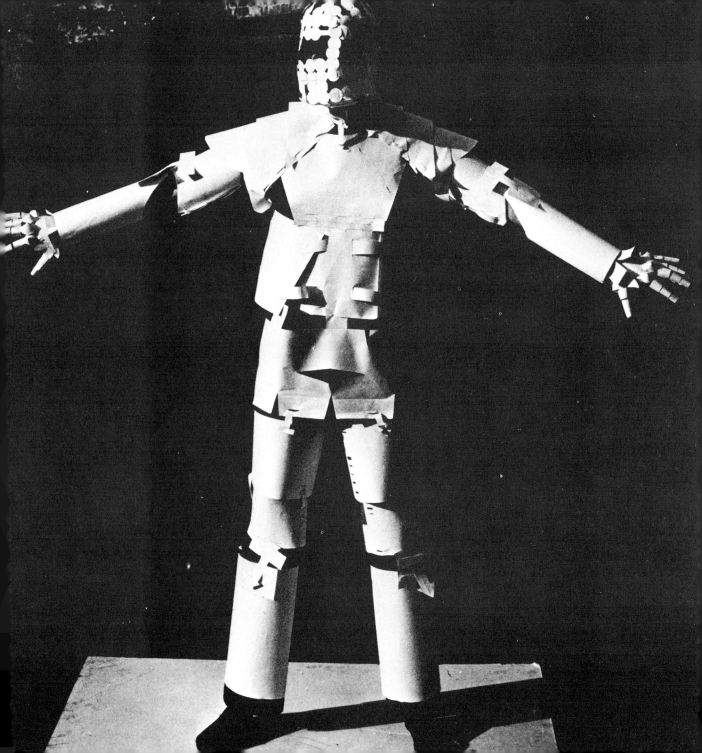

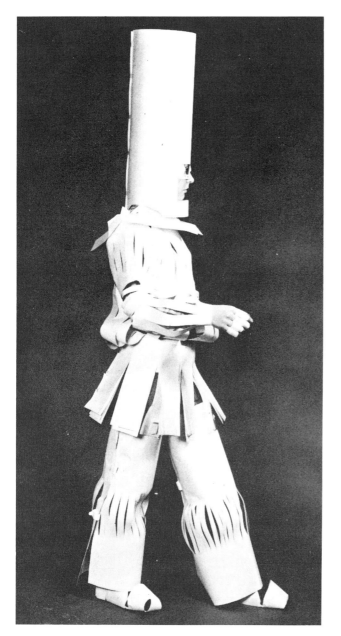
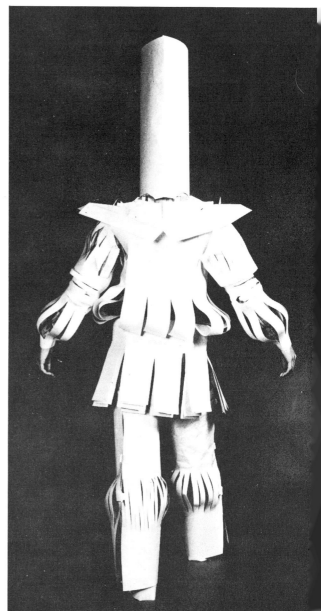

opposite
30, 31 This costume has an overall feeling of
simplicity. The sheets of paper have been slashed
vertically, except the sleeves which were also slashed
horizontally and then folded into tubes of varying
sizes

32 This garment appears to be rather congested
and frivolous without the continuity of one particular
shape or series of shapes right through the garment

overleaf
33 The two costumes together give a strong
contrast of both shape and texture

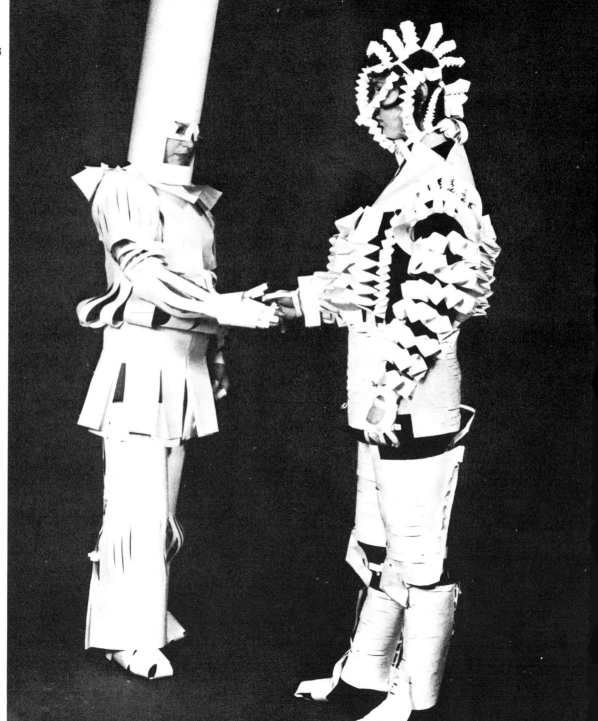

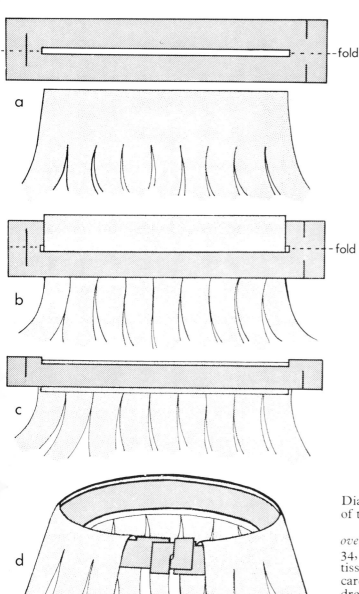

Diagram 23   The basic method of assembling layers of tissue paper on to a cardboard band

overleaf

34, 35   This costume has been constructed out of tissue paper, which has been mounted on to bands of card. The colours ranged from yellow on the head dress, through shades of orange on the body and finally to red around the leg sections. This garment 'floated' when the model moved around the room

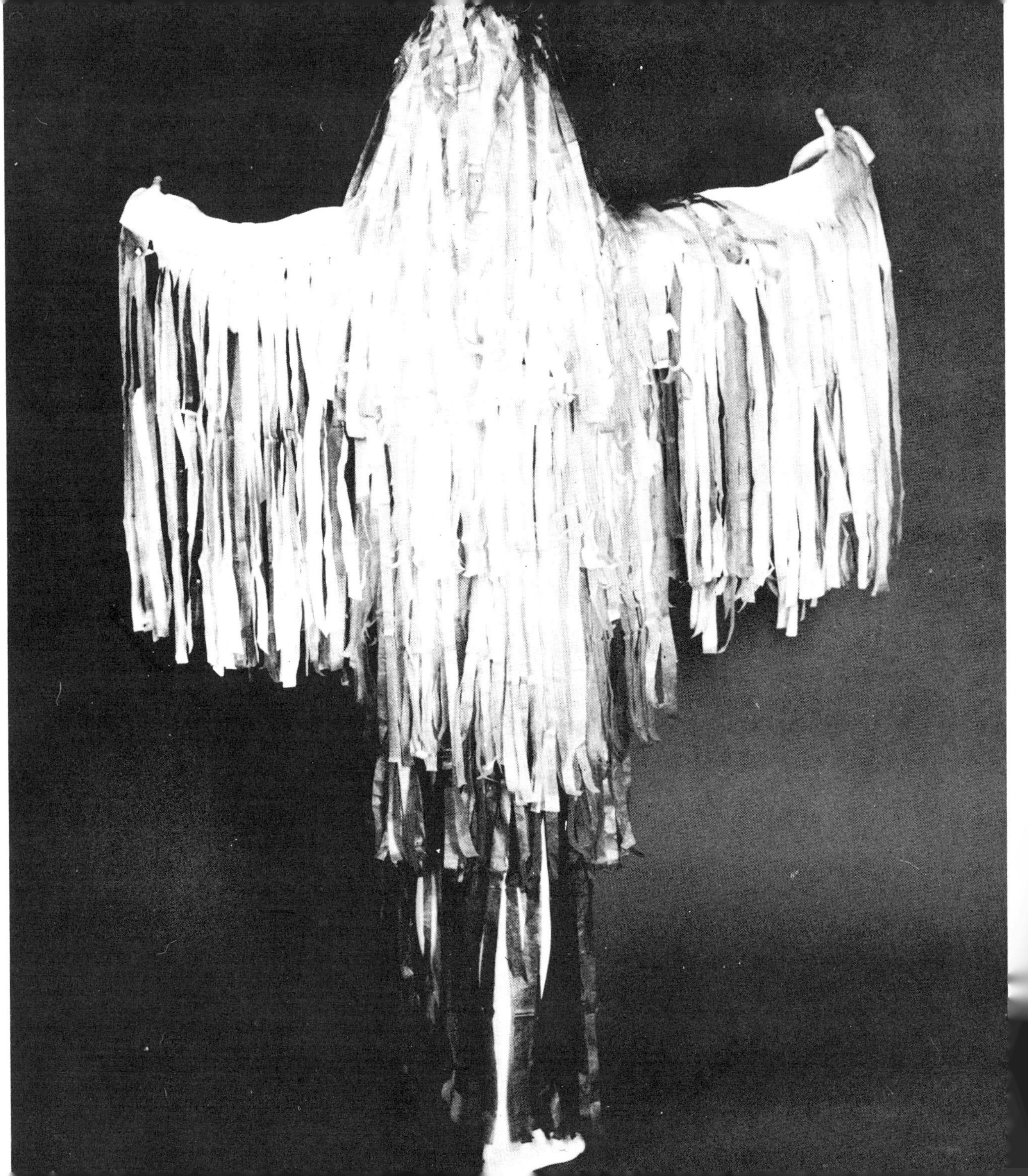

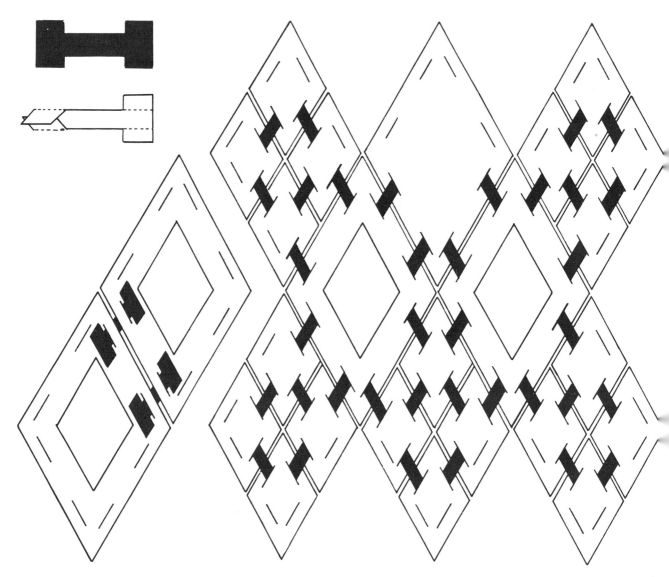

Diagram 24   Construction of a section of a garment with its method of linking

36, 37   Total full scale covering. This garment has been made out of cartridge paper which has been covered with kitchen foil, then cut to shape and linked together

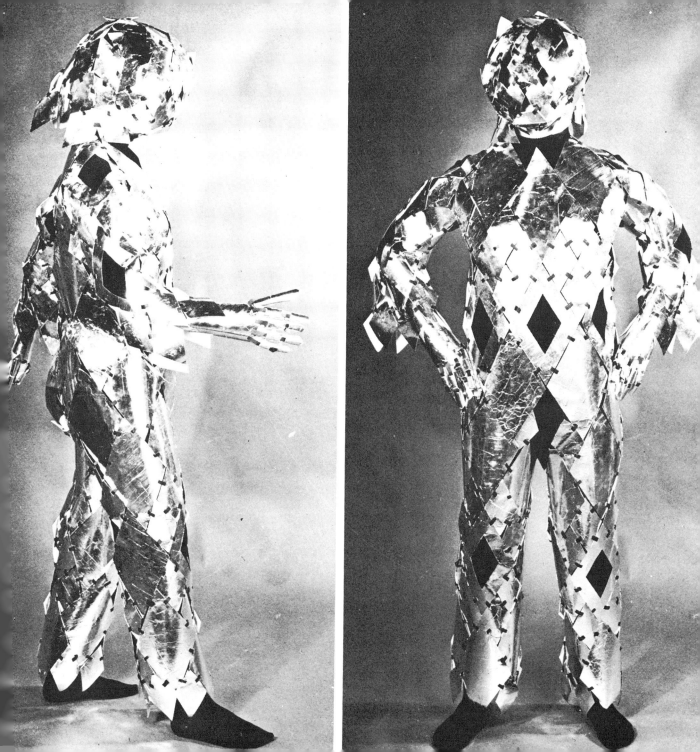

38, 39 This garment shows a gathering together of
the ideas of different people which have been unified
by colour (red and white) and by the weight of the
cartridge paper which has been used for each
section

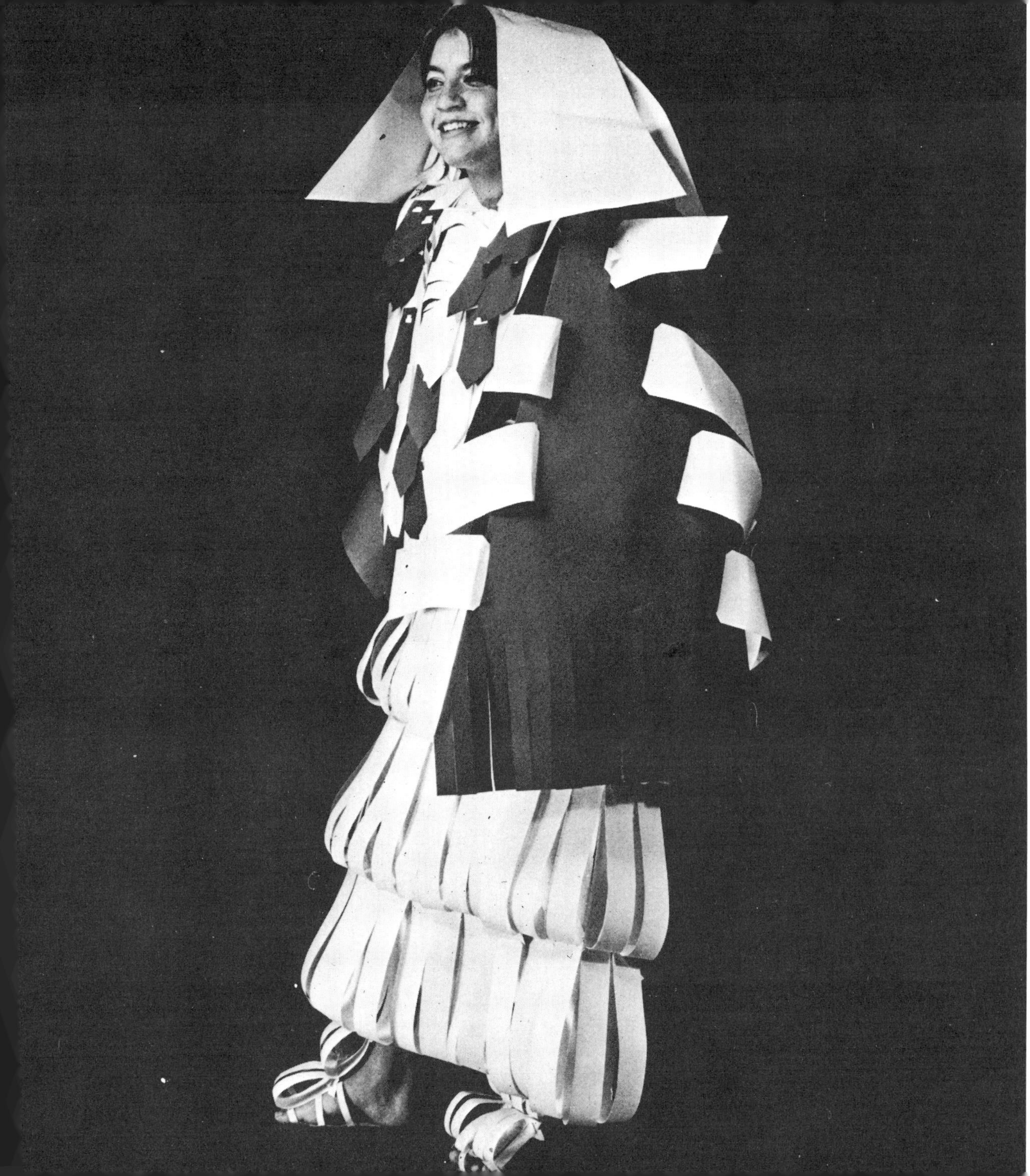

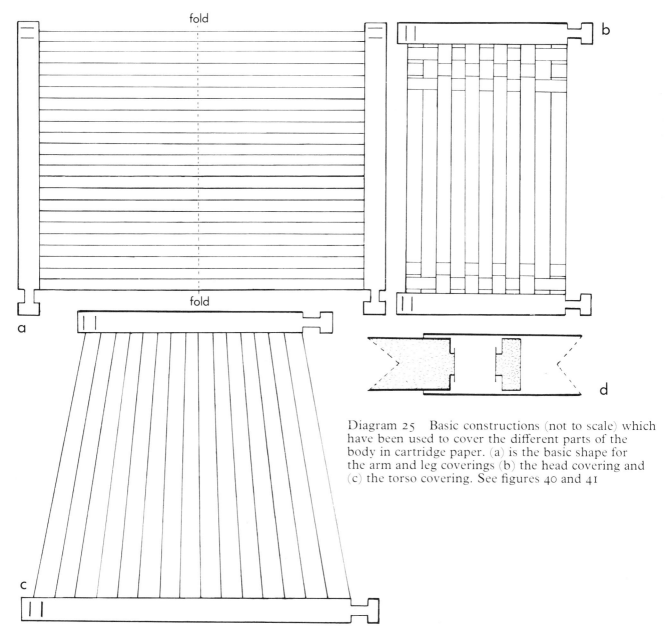

fold

fold

a

b

c

d

Diagram 25   Basic constructions (not to scale) which
have been used to cover the different parts of the
body in cartridge paper. (a) is the basic shape for
the arm and leg coverings (b) the head covering and
(c) the torso covering. See figures 40 and 41

right and overleaf
40, 41   The costume shows the white cartridge
paper construction in full scale. See colour plate 4
facing page 77

overleaf
lates 2 and 3   A costume of kitchen foil over
ewspaper and cartridge paper. This reflective
arment has been decorated with applied
uorescent shapes, in very bright colours and has
een created to be worn under ultra-violet lighting

61

41

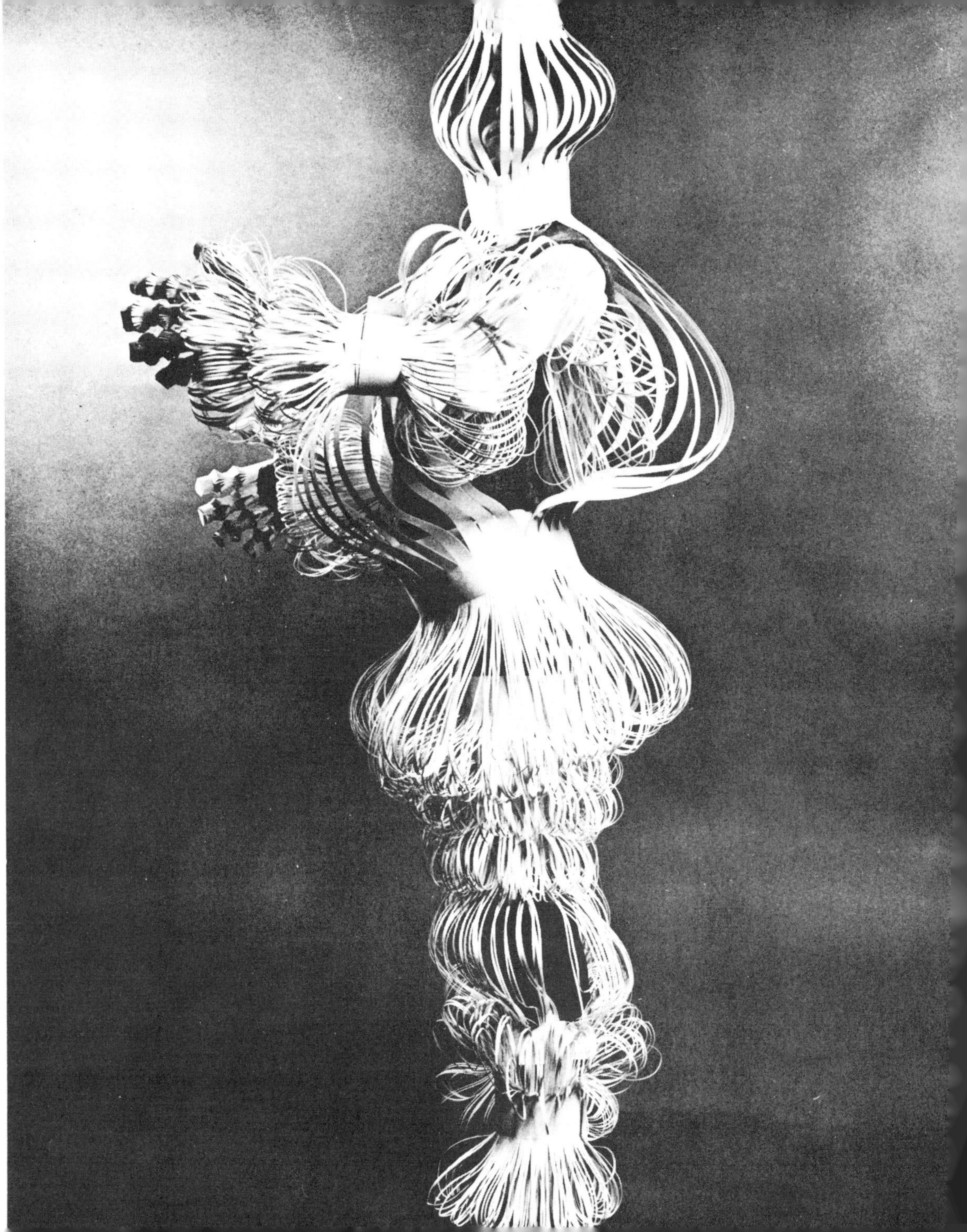

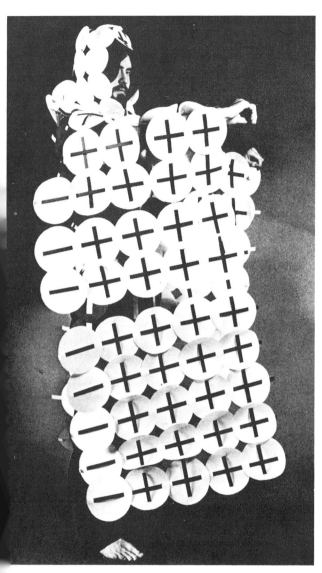

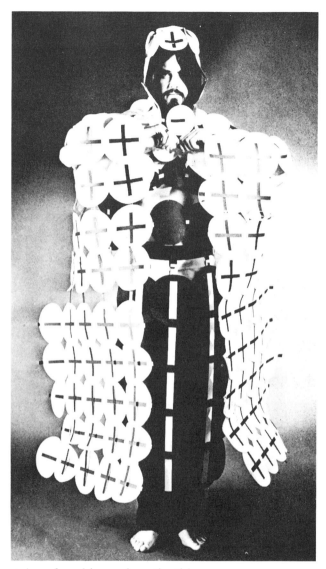

42, 43 and 44 *overleaf* This garment is a construction of paper circles which have been laced together by strips of card which have been threaded through one circle and then through to another. The strips of card have given the thin paper some stability whilst at the same time keeping the overall construction very light in weight

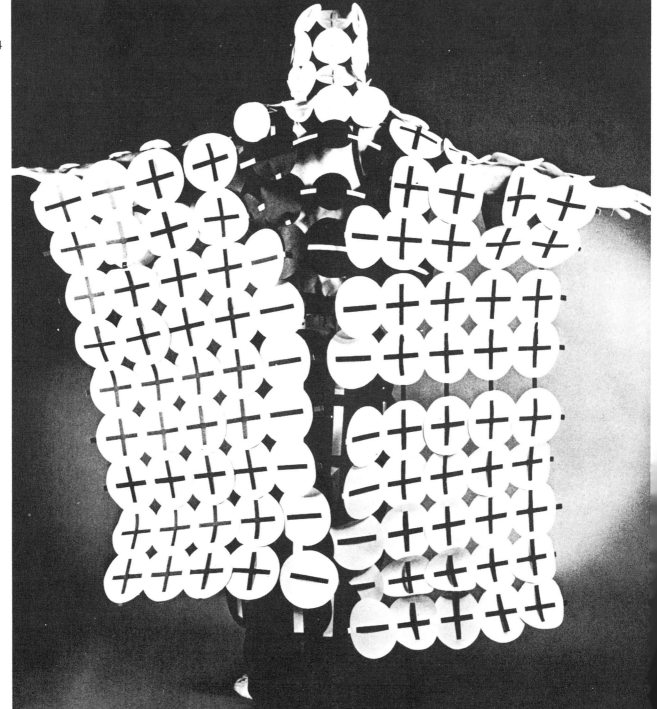

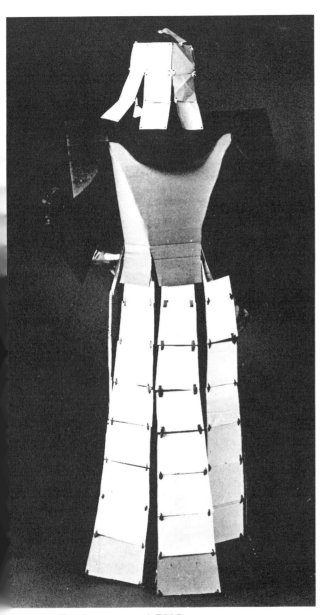
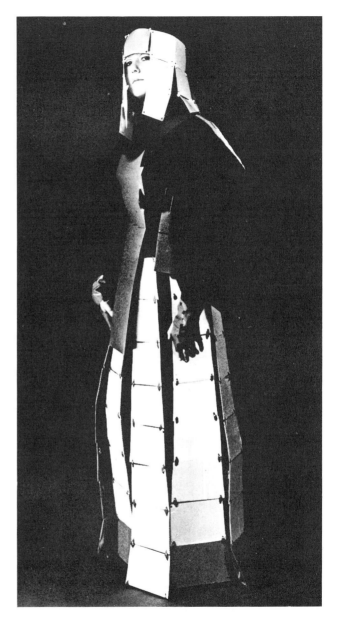

45, 46   Card, paper and PVC costume

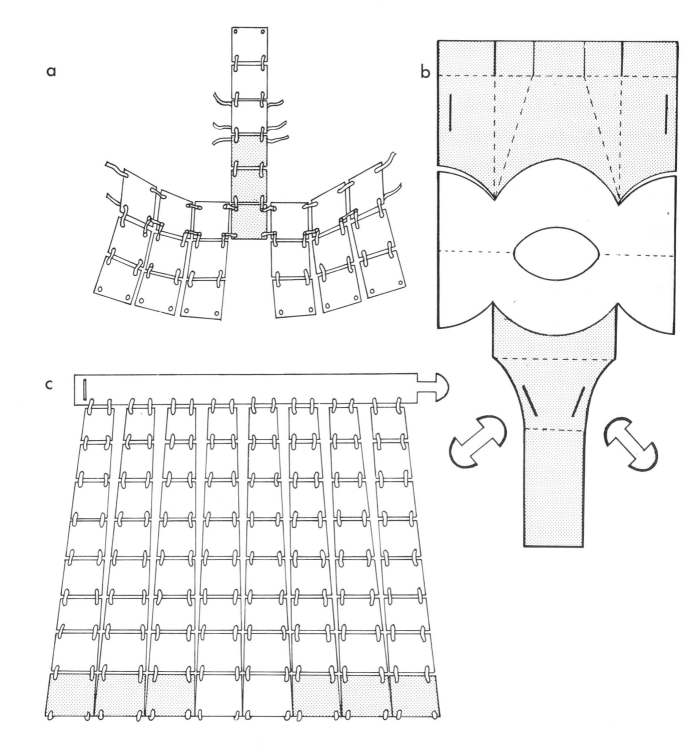

a

b

c

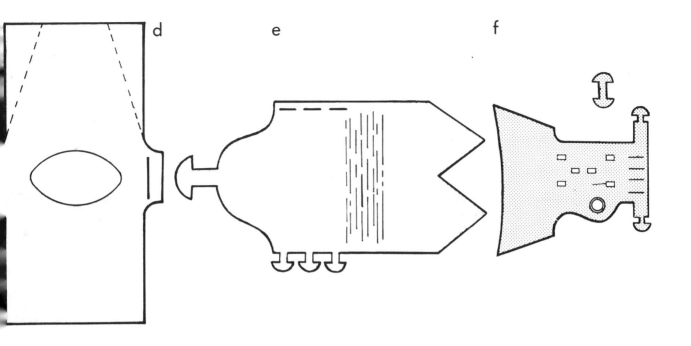

Diagrams 26 and 27   Basic construction of the card, paper and PVC costume. (The drawings are not to scale)

(a)   The head dress has been constructed from paper squares which are laced together by twisted paper 'string'

(b)   The shoulder to waist covering, back and front with the separate linking units. This has been constructed from corrugated card and the shoulder sections covered with paper

(c)   The skirt part of the costume, constructed out of corrugated card and laced together by strips of PVC

(d)   The paper under-vest back and front

(e)   This paper arm section links to section (d) as indicated

(f)   The wrist and hand covering with the additional finger linking tab constructed in PVC

67

47 An experiment in using fluorescent papers to form a multi-coloured tabard and helmet, to be worn specifically under ultra-violet lighting. See colour plate 1 facing page 44

opposite
48 Black card and metallic PVC costume

48

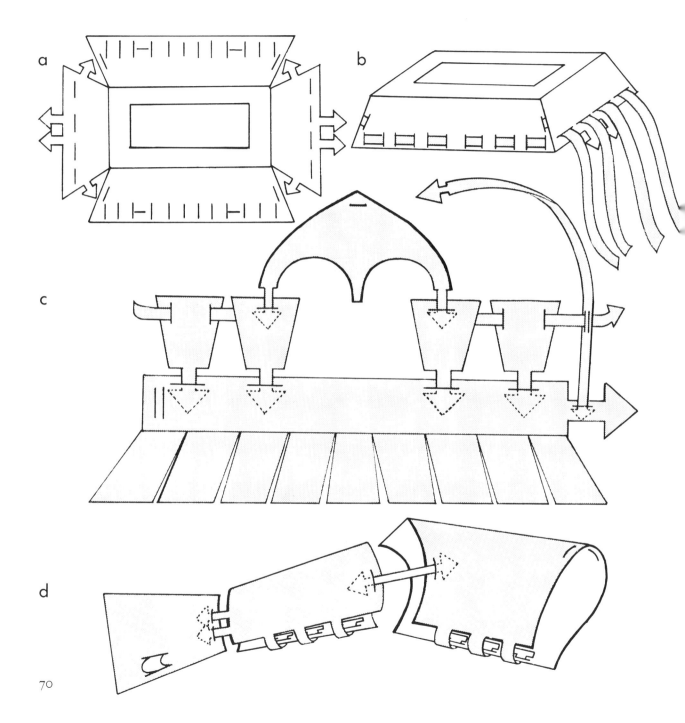

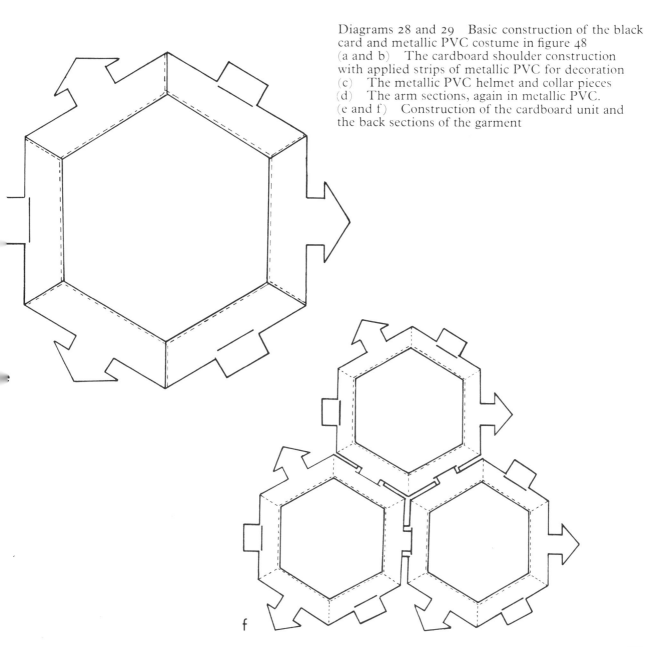

Diagrams 28 and 29   Basic construction of the black
card and metallic PVC costume in figure 48
(a and b)   The cardboard shoulder construction
with applied strips of metallic PVC for decoration
(c)   The metallic PVC helmet and collar pieces
(d)   The arm sections, again in metallic PVC.
(e and f)   Construction of the cardboard unit and
the back sections of the garment

f

BODICE DETAILS

 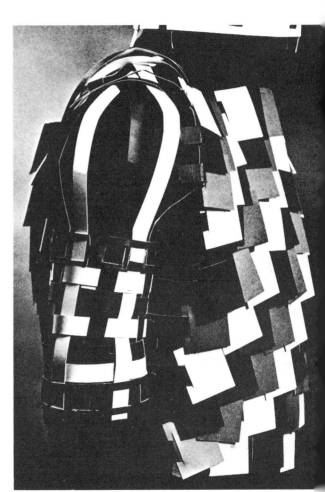

49, 50   This garment has been constructed from
medium weight card in three different colours, which
has been slotted together and interwoven

opposite

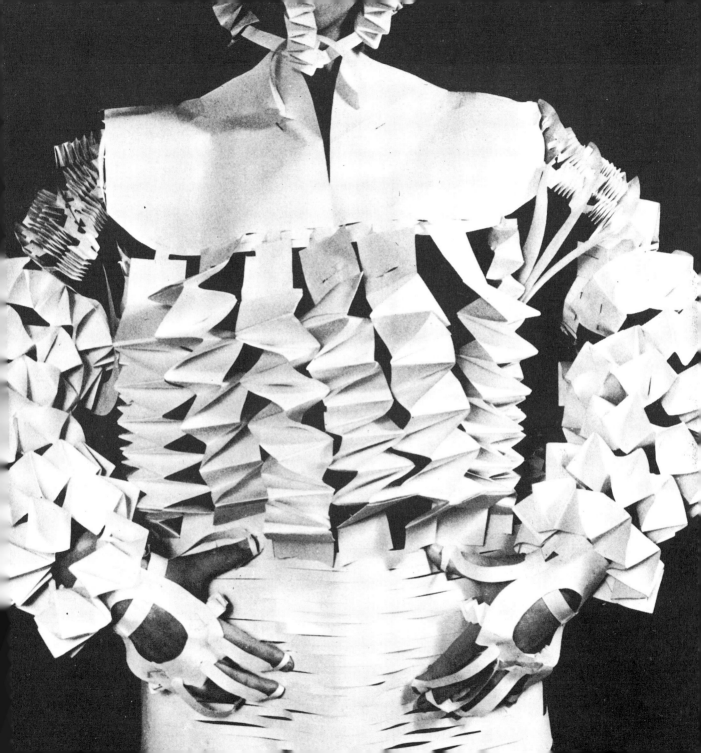

52, 53 This costume has been constructed out of sugar paper which has been folded, cut, interlocked and woven

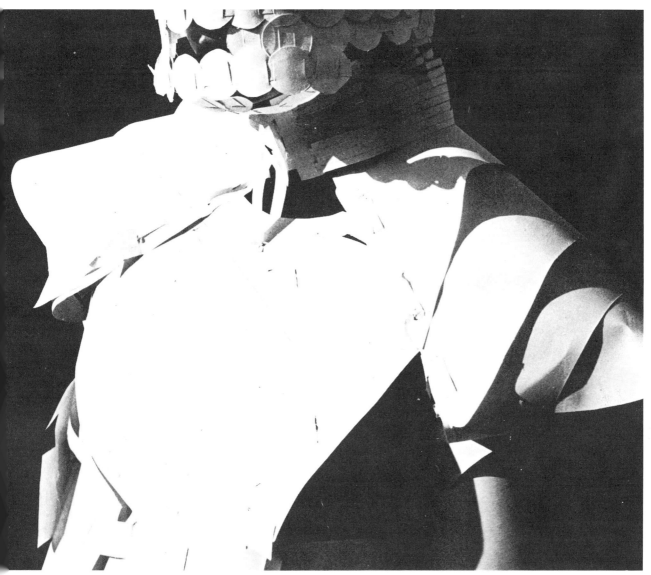

4   White cartridge paper has been carefully cut and
ced to its adjoining sections

HEAD COVERINGS

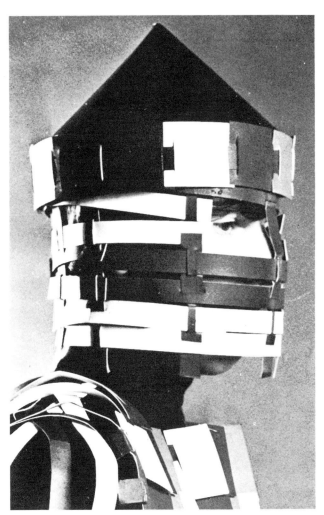

55   Interwoven stiff card in three colours

56   Folded and woven strips of sugar paper

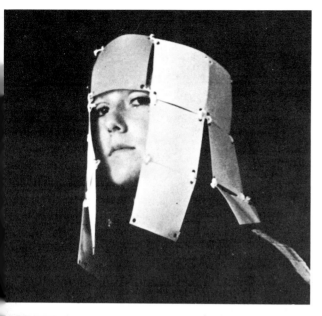

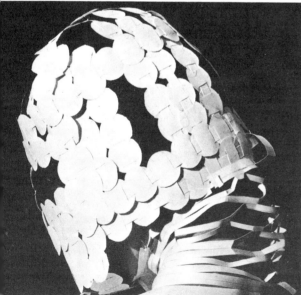

above left
47   Cartridge paper squares and rolled paper 'string' used to lace the squares together

above right
48   Curled strips of cartridge paper were mounted on to a card frame. The paper strips were curled by being pulled slowly and tightly over a pair of scissors

left
50   White cartridge paper, slotted and laced

opposite
Plate 4(a)   The costume shows the white cartridge paper construction in full scale. See page 61

Plate 4(b)   Kitchen foil over cartridge paper costume. Created to be worn under strong white light in order to give a high reflection

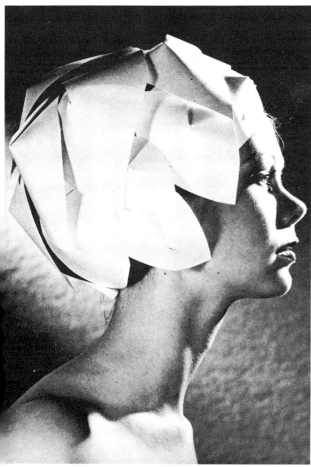

60 to 63   The framework for the two head-dresses
was constructed by bending strips of cardboard of
varying lengths but approximately 30 mm in width
round a wooden hat block and then stapling together
the strips at points where they overlapped. Fringed
strips of paper were stapled piece by piece in varying
lengths on one framework and different sized petal
like shapes on the other. The many different weights
and colours of paper which can be obtained could
all be used in a variety of shapes on this basic
framework

HAND COVERINGS

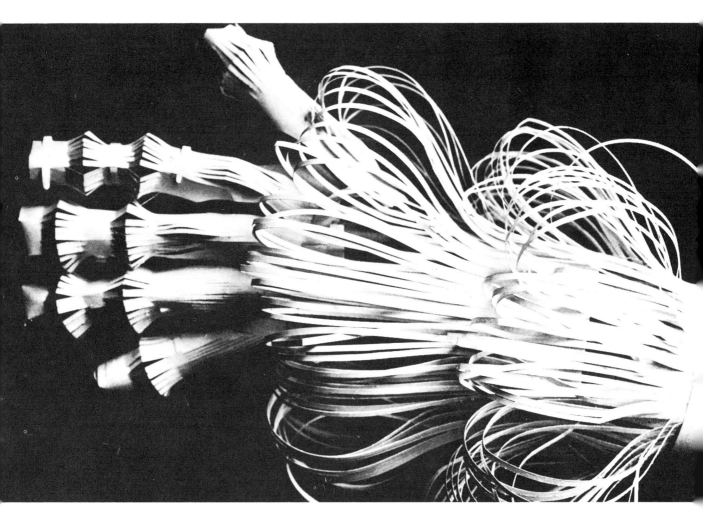

64 Lacerated and folded cartridge paper

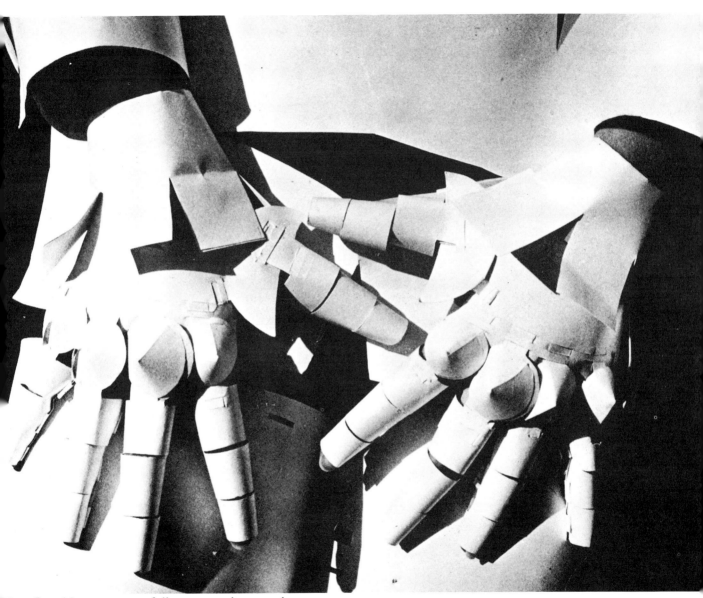

5   Cartridge paper carefully measured, cut and
folded and based on a study of armour

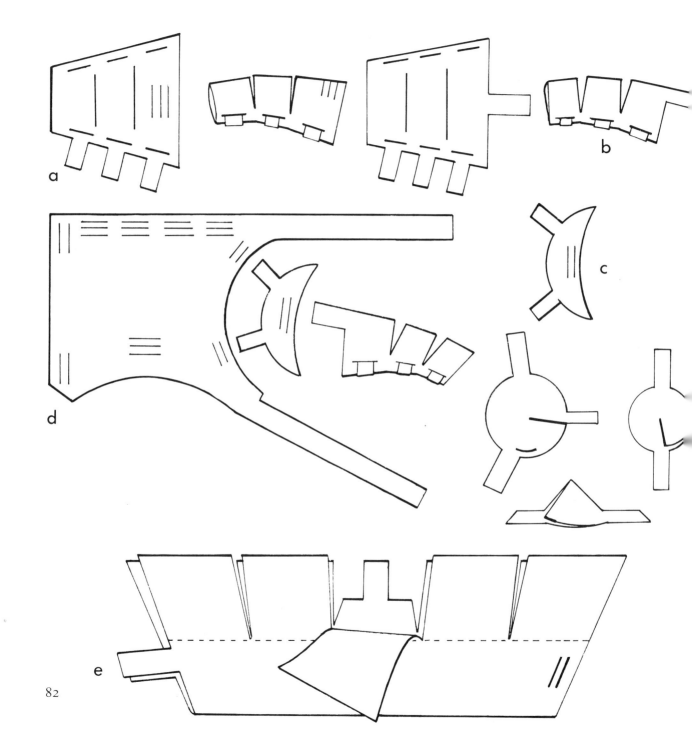

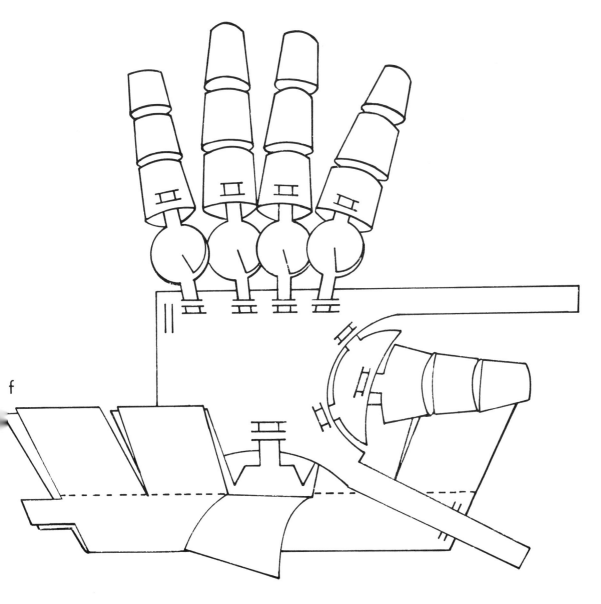

f

Diagrams 30 and 31 The construction of figure 65:
the different sections are linked together by the tab
and slot device to make up a complete hand unit.
(a) Finger unit
(b) Thumb unit

(c) Knuckle units
(d) Hand unit
(e) Wrist unit
(f) Complete hand with finger units, showing tab
and slot linking

Decoration

Decoration can be applied before, or after the garment has been fully constructed.

Decorating the sheets of paper or card before construction gives the advantage of being able to apply the paint to a flat surface. This makes spraying around a shape or through doilies etc very easy.

Motifs can be applied by a screen print to the flat card or paper or an all over design can be applied by this method.

Applying pressure whilst sticking on shapes whether delicate or made of stiff card is much easier when the basic structure of a garment is flat.

The disadvantages are that unless very accurate measuring has taken place the sprayed on motifs or applied decorations could be in the wrong place, out of line or out of context when the entire garment is put together. It is easy to overdecorate when the garment is flat and then end up with a confused rather messy finished object.

However, the random placing of shapes when the garment is in the flat and in pieces can often create a startling effect when the final costume is assembled and often the element of chance produces some very good results. Decorating the finished garment when it has been assembled on the model or on a dress stand has its advantages. It is easy to see where the motif or applied decoration should go. If a good contact adhesive is used there should be little problem in applying shapes of different sizes and weights.

Problems can arise when applying paint in this situation and great care must be taken to prevent the paint from running. Also, it is much easier to unite painted shapes such as continuous lines or stripes on a completely assembled garment.

Points to remember
when scoring or lacerating paper, PVC and acetate

Always use a sharp cutting blade, a metal ruler, and a cutting board or a thick piece of card underneath the paper. Keep fingers away from the blade area. Hold the knife firmly and draw it along the surface of the paper slowly, using the metal ruler for straight lines or free-hand for curves.

For a clear sharp fold or bend in a piece of card, score the surface of the card lightly, breaking the surface only with the cutting blade. Then bend the card into position.

When folding any paper or card, if the fold line is complicated then, for greater accuracy, mark the desired shape on the paper first.

Press each fold line firmly either by drawing the thumb or a ruler along the folded edge.

Strips of paper can be easily curled by pulling one end of the strip tightly over the back of a pair or scissors or ruler, then gently but firmly drawing the paper over the ruler or scissors from one end to the other. When the tension is released the paper should spring into a fairly tight spiral.

Each different type of paper will produce a different type of curl. Generally, cartridge paper gives a stiffly shaped curl which has plenty of bounce.

COSTUMES IN PVC

Polythene and household PVCs are obtainable in many colours and surface textures.

Sheets of polythene and PVC can be handled in the same way as large sheets of paper, although neither material can be glued together successfully. However, a satisfactory result can be obtained by using the edge of a household iron set at a medium heat. It is important to have a special barrier strip or a piece of paper placed between the edge of the iron and the pieces of polythene. By moving the edge of the iron slowly along the barrier strip, the edges of polythene underneath will fuse together by the heat transmitted.

For PVC simple mechanical methods can be both successful and decorative. These include: tap-on rivets; eyelets and lacing; staples: PVC-backed adhesive tape; *Sellotape* or *Scotch Tape*; adhesive patches, sold in a variety of colours and used to mend small punctures.

It is important to remember that polythene and PVC can cause suffocation if worn too close to the body. Therefore, if a head covering is to be made the mouth and nose should be left unrestricted. Slits or decoratively punched holes allow the air to enter and circulate inside the costume.

56   A garment constructed from household PVC. The PVC has been handled as sheets of paper and each section is held in place by tap-on rivets which snap together

85

67   Samples of knitted PVC

left
Diagram 32   Method of cutting a sheet of PVC into strips so that it can be used for knitting

opposite
68   This dress and hat have been knitted in extruded transparent PVC of approximately 2.5 mm in diameter. Fine silver lurex thread has been introduced in places in order to reduce the transparency and to increase the sparkle of the garment